DAVID THORPE

JUN HASEGAWA

DEXTER DALWOOD

PETER DAVIES

GARY WEBB

SHAUN ROBERTS

GILBERT McCARRAGHER

MICHAEL RAEDECKER

CAROLINE WARDE

JANE BRENNAN

MARTIN MALONEY

STEVEN GONTARSKI

DIE YOUNG STAY PRETTY

Institute of Contemporary Arts, London
13 November 1998 - 10 January 1999

ISBN 1-900300-15-X

UK and Europe:
ICA Exhibitions
12 Carlton House Terrace
London SW1Y 5AH

Distributed by
Cornerhouse Publications
70 Oxford Street
Manchester M1 5NH

Published by the ICA to coincide with the exhibition Die Young Stay Pretty, 13 November
1998 - 10 January 1999, Lower and Upper Galleries, Institute of Contemporary Arts.

Die Young Stay Pretty has been curated by Martin Maloney.

The ICA would like to thank Martin Maloney and the artists for their great enthusiasm and
support without which this exhibition could not have taken place: Jane Brennan, Caroline
Warde, Jun Hasegawa, Dexter Dalwood, David Thorpe, Peter Davies, Shaun Roberts, Gilbert
McCarragher, Michael Raedecker, Gary Webb and Steven Gontarski. We would also like to thank
the writers for their contributions and the artists for their interviews. Finally we are
most grateful to the Anthony D'Offay Gallery, the Saatchi Gallery and Jake Miller/The
Approach for their kind collaboration in this exhibition.

© the artists, Patricia Ellis, Gemma de Cruz, Martin Maloney, Emma Dexter, ICA, 1998.

Printed by The Pale Green Press

Institute of Contemporary Arts, The Mall
London SW1Y 5AH
Tel(44) (0)171 930 0493 Fax (44) (0)171 873 0051
e-mail:info@ica.org.uk
Web site:http://www.illumin.co.uk/ica

Registered charity number 236848

Director: Philip Dodd
Director of Exhibitions: Emma Dexter
Exhibitions Organisers: Katya García-Antón and Susan Copping
Gallery Manager: Angus Howie
Exhibitions Interns: Zoe Bingham, Justin McGuirk and Ariella Yedgar

Die Young Stay Pretty is sponsored by Habitat habitat

The ICA is grateful to acknowledge the support of the British Council

The ICA is financially assisted by The Arts Council of England, Westminster City Council
and the British Film Institute.

Die Young Stay Pretty is an exhibition curated especially for the ICA by an artist, Martin Maloney. Maloney has been an energetic proponent on the London scene of a return to figuration, to retinal pleasure and the joys of making things with the hands. This exhibition, its feel and mood, reflect Maloney's own eclectic creative spirit.

Maloney came to prominence in 1995 when he set up a gallery in his Brixton flat called Lost in Space and presented a series of group exhibitions with catchy titles like Multiple Orgasm or White Trash. Intrepid art lovers beat a path to deepest South London where they were treated to chaotic, charmingly installed exhibitions.

Maloney and his peers have been educated in London, formally at art school and informally through the exhibitions they have visited and the magazines they have consumed. I first met Maloney in 1992 at a seminar at Goldsmiths College on the ICA True Stories exhibition, which developed a cult following amongst students and young artists. That was the first show in London to let 'teen art' out of the bag: Karen Kilimnik, Raymond Pettibon, Jim Shaw and Jack Pierson created complex works that referenced the full gamut of US suburban subculture: violence, beauty, drugs, religion, suffused with a romantic spirit and an obsessive manner. Often the aesthetic was abject and scatter, or it employed handy but humdrum methods - drawings, snapshots and small paintings.

Six years later that teen angst is transfigured in Die Young Stay Pretty with the addition of grandiose art-historical inspirations that would normally be considered off-limits for young artists: Michelangelo, Claude Lorraine, Poussin and Klimt provide new and fertile ground for investigation. The work has a distinctly formal feel, any hint of installation has gone.

In addition to orchestrating the exhibition Maloney has been the inspiration for the catalogue, commissioning the interviews with the artists and Patricia Ellis's unusual and wide-ranging essay. I would like to take this opportunity to express my own and the ICA's thanks to Martin Maloney for his vision and hard work and to the artists for their dedication and enthusiasm for the show. I would also like to thank our enlightened sponsors Habitat who have made the exhibition possible and who are themselves doing so much to create new audiences and opportunities for artists.

How Soon is Now?[1]
Patricia Ellis

Just pull on your pout
and let's move to the beat like we know that it's over...[2]

Then Trend:

Flashback: Bitter Sweet Languor is the crux for the most eloquent of teenage fantasies. The destiny-melodrama of un-requited first love, being chronically misunderstood, never fitting in. Sulky Seduction. Vicariously romanticising your own awkwardness through Fashion Trauma, this is youth glamour at it's best: The Breakfast Club,[3] Rules of Attraction,[4] 21 Jump Street,[5] The Smiths.[6] Clean-cut pouty boys, pop-goth, hair gel, River Phoenix. Fabrication fixation: this is a generation of monetarily liquid, unisexual, naïve nihilism. Image is everything.

Now:

Die Young Stay Pretty embraces all these feelings of decadence. 80s kids in the wake of the Millennium,[7] introjected pop-culture racing against time. Trend-casualties of the heroic century.[8] Bigger Faster Better: these artists slide effortlessly through space and time. Unlike the Karen Kilimniks and Larry Johnsons before them, these artists are not in awe of sensation overload. They master it readily, they surf it. Teetering on the edge of the future: Romance is all the rage. Rampant imagination: Bionic men, on-line dating, X-files[9]. Enchantment in the everyday. Science Fiction Fact. (tv)Image addiction: escalating competition to build the more perfect image, Beauty is an act of obsession, an endeavour of love. The image is the idea. Emotion is numb.

---

[1] ..."When you say it's going to happen Now, when exactly do you mean? 'Cause I've already waited too long, and all my hope is gone..." The Smiths, *How Soon is Now*, <u>*Hatful of Hollow*</u>, 1984.

[2] **The Cure,** *Fascination Street*, <u>*Disintegration*</u>, **1989**. 80s teen-paean extraordinaire. Fabulous angst-ridden lyrics like..."Cos I'm paling and I'm beggin' you to drag you down with me to kick the last nail in..."

[3] A Misfit, an Athlete, a Princess, a Rebel, well, you know how it goes… Cuter-than-buttons: Ally Sheedy, Emilio Estevez and the rest of the Brat Pack spend Saturday in detention coming to terms with their stressful suburban realities. They smoke some grass, dance to some Kenny Loggins and Molly does the trick with the lip-gloss. The John Hughes Classic with that Simple Minds theme song.

[4] Novelist American-Psycho Brett Easton Ellis and the Troubled Teen. Lots of sex, shopping and cocaine. Ellis's top ten list of ***Why Kids Are Ruining America*** can be found at: **http://www.adingoatemybaby.com/whykidsareruining.html**

[5] Dependency-inducing TV series (1987-90) starring pre-fame Johnny Depp and son-of-Dom Peter DeLuise. Obviously grown-up undercover cops disguise themselves as teenagers to infiltrate West Coast High Schools, cracking endless scores of adolescent crime rings.

[6] The Top 40 apotheosis of melodrama with major hits like ***Heaven Knows I'm Miserable Now, Girlfriend in a Coma, Death of a Disco Dancer.*** (*Please read in the voice of your mother: *What's the matter with you? Why don't you listen to something <u>happy</u>?*)

[7] Speaking of 80s and the Millennium, did you know Bill and Hillary Clinton have hired **Steven Spielberg** and **Quincy Jones** to design the White House New Year's Eve party? (Like Bill's gonna be there!)

[8] The Hero is the over-achievement of the 20th century. Henry Ford (automotive hero) to Dr. George Washington Carver (peanut butter hero), Charlie Chaplin (funny hero) to Mother Teresa (not so funny hero), Yury Gagarin (outerspace hero) to Bill Borroughs (innerspace hero), Foucault (smart hero) to Tanya Harding (anti-hero). Not to mention Xena, William Katt (***The Greatest American Hero***), the Hero sandwich, the Gyros and millions and billions of others.

[9] Love stories of the 90s: The Viagra option; Virtual Couples whisper sweet nothings in small font; The slow realisation that Scully and Mulder will NEVER have an on-screen kiss. Flirtation: the potential for romance is far more compelling than actual participation.

<u>Style 2000:</u>

Dexter Dalwood, David Thorpe, Michael Raedecker, Jane Brennan, Caroline Warde, Peter Davies, Jun Hasegawa, Gary Webb, Steven Gontarski, Martin Maloney and **Shaun Roberts/Gilbert McCarragher** have each devoured this media gluttony. Weaned on TV, joysticks and fashion magazines, they are hysteria-savvy, casually interacting with sensationalism. In the apocalyptic approach of 2000,[10] these artists leisurely domesticate the commodity blitz. Their hand-made aesthetic intimates their simulated realities, digital nostalgia: sentimentalising the numb. Suburban-star-victims of a virtual age. Tragically hip, their work is posed: beautiful, profound, seductive, edged with just enough trauma to make it truly glamorous.

The countdown begins...

5.

He knows where he's taking me,
taking me where I want to be...I hope he never lets me down again[11]

To **David Thorpe** and **Dexter Dalwood** ambience is crucial. Imaging settings for the most indulgent fantasies, Thorpe and Dalwood re-create the aura of luxury from non-memory. The sensation of film, advertising, Jackie Collins[12] novels is recreated, shared, like personal experience, first hand knowledge.

Dalwood's paintings are canny renderings of famous places he has never seen. *Paisley Park,*[13] *Sharon Tate's House.*[14] Shrouded in mystery they are nevertheless iconographic in collective imagination. The Hockney-esque[15] style of Laboratoire Garnier satiates all expectations: chrome, glass, pristine cosmetic shades. This is an invented scene worthy of Dynasty's Linda Evans.[16] A luxury spa, a chemist's lab. Money and Corruption: this is a place where nature is reversed. Impossible\believable because of its soap opera associations.[17]

---

[10] If you don't believe me, go to the Nostradamus homepage for detailed 1999 predictions i.e. The Anti-Christ's plan for a Unified Monetary System, Our Death by Radio Waves, etc. Really scary stuff.
http://www.cis.ohio-state.edu/hypertext/faq/usenet/nostradamus/top.html

[11] **Depeche Mode,** *Never Let Me Down Again*, <u>**Music for the Masses**</u>, **1987.**

[12] Sister to ***Dynasty***'s Alexis, Jackie maintains the legendary Collins style. Best-selling grocery store smut, i.e. <u>**Hollywood Wives**</u> and <u>**Rock Star**</u>, supposedly fictionalise the real-lives of celebrities (who of course exist only in the hermetically sealed world of five-star hotels and beach front homes with pools).

[13] ..."**U don't have 2 watch Dynasty 2 have an attitude...**" TAFKAPrince's Minneapolis Sound Studio is almost as notorious as Mr. <u>**1999**</u> himself, spawning such 80s sexsations as The Time, Apollo 6 and Sheila E. Contemporary Paisley Park Soundstage clients include Burger King, Comet Cleanser, Volkswagon, the Beastie Boys, Hammer, Stevie Ray Vaughn, Neil Young, Kool & The Gang, the Muppets, the Bee Gees, Barry Manilow, and Jeff Beck.
http://www.bitstream.net/paisleypark/ The sound stage can be rented for $125 an hour. Technical help is $15/hr extra. This includes hair salon and showers.

[14] <u>*Helter Skelter*</u> lore: the site of the infamous Sharon Tate murders by the Manson Family has been shown over and over again. In photos, on TV, in film. Reconstructing, retelling, the space is as blank in our memory as all the rest of the details of the trial.

[15] Love that California-Hockney. Oooh, A Bigger Splash please!

[16] "'At the beginning of the show, you saw only the legs of the woman. Then the body. At the end, panting viewers were let into the secret. It was Linda Evans. Actually, it wasn't Linda Evans. The legs were those of actress Anna Leigh London. The body was of Quin Kessler. The foot and leg model [said]: "I have tiny legs and feet that don't look anything like Linda's. I have a size four foot. Linda is a beautiful woman but I think her feet are size eight or eight and a half.' Yes and she also has bunions..." **Excerpt from: Freedland, Michael, <u>Linda Evans</u>, UK: Weidenfeld & Nicolson, 1986, pp. 178-9.**

[17] Somewhere in these buildings there is always a captive of a mad doctor or a criminal getting a new face.

The splendorous landscapes in David Thorpe's collages also resonate a familiar genre of Style. From Seurat to Katz, Thorpe tempers clean savoir-faire with celluloid repose. Vast expanses of nature, glamorized by the seductive glow of neon lights; These isolated urban tableaux are lavish settings for lovers, delicious scenes for crime. Intricately pieced together from construction paper, Thorpe languidly recreates the sublime; Elaborate perfection, these scenes are more fascinating than the real.

Longingly re-creating ultimate leisure and glamour: representations of Ideal, resoundingly, passionately empty.

9.

I almost believe that the pictures are all I can feel[18]

Michael Raedecker, **Jane Brennan** and **Caroline Warde** capitalise on the idyllic concept of nature. Their representations of landscape and still life corrupt the traditional intentions of these genres. Redefining romanticism, these artists commodify ecology, recreating it as something *Urban*, manufactured. The organic becomes an item of Warhol-ized inanimation.

Raedecker's painting tactilely modernise the history of robust verve-ish landscapes. The essence of America: these John-Wayne-outdoor scenes are muted with the colours of suburbia, embroidered with the element of granny-craft. Clichéd, fashion plated, these rural splendours become vapid, synthesised. Raedecker manipulates his landscapes into something *made*, unnatural, something which can be adored.

Jane Brennan's paintings, *Nightingale* and *Beads* are simplistically elegant. Delicate, flawless, astringently sentimental. The ardor in these images is genuine, the devotion to beauty absolute. Isolating, cherishing, improving, preserving; These images lie somewhere between girlhood confection and Victorian collection(death) mania.[19] Brennan's still lives freeze the temporal. This is a love everlasting.

Almost Religious: Caroline Warde's still lives inject a bit of gothic punk into the idea of the natural. *Peach Branch*: Styled like 16th century Dürer etc. etchings, this fruit is truly forbidden; black, plastic, perverse, sexual. Chemical-Equestrian, *Mule* is seamless, sumptuous, suffocating. Toxic fetishism is the fashion: the still life is enslaved in a leather-culture positure. Complete adulteration of the subtle *morte* reminders of traditional still life: Immortality is the 21st century vogue.

Treasured and lifeless as pressed leaves or dried flowers, Raedecker, Brennan and Warde do much more than pay homage to landscape. They cryonise[20]/canonise it. Forever preserved as tokens of Beauty, objects of affection.

---

[18] **The Cure, *Pictures Of You*, <u>Disintegration</u>. 1989.** As far removed from nature as humanly possible, dyed black hair and smeared lipstick can make even Robert Smith look great.

[19] You know, these prudish collections of bugs and birds and flowers and etchings and pretty much anything that could be preserved behind glass with a tiny quill-penned label. Interior decor, intellectual pretension and sexual repression all in the name of Science. **Tourist advice: Check out the Pitt Rivers Museum in Oxford. Tel: (01865) 270927**

[20] Cryogenics can be used for freezing something in liquid helium-4 (-238(F) at the precise moment of death so that it may be preserved for later resurrection. i.e. Walt Disney's head.

3.

Ground control to Major Tom
take your protein pills and put your helmet on[21]

Digitally influenced. **Jun Hasegawa** and **Peter Davies** merge the beauty of craft with the perfection of image. Painting, the most passionate of activities, aptly captures the tragic romance of the typical(topical).

Peter Davies's text and abstract paintings dwell in the fantastic and deficient. Escher-esque black and white graphic designs repeat to infinity. Wonky and home-made, these patternings feel oddly historical: tender reminders of naïve beginnings in technographics, TV screen hypnosis, special effects, drug culture. Portraying ancient ideas of tomorrow, space-race dreams and James Bond futurism. Utopia-Imagination not yet fully realised. Desire: hopeful, naïve…futile.

Hasegawa's celebrity portraits share the look of sexy Japanimation vixens. Movie-waif *Juliette Lewis* and Style Council's *Young Paul Weller* are painted in comic book format, generified beyond recognition: Lichtensteins for Y2K. With the invention of cyber-celebs *(Lara*[22] *et al.)*, even these young stars have become outdated/obsolete. Hasegawa's paintings supersede their real counterparts. Exceeding their limitations. Extending semiotics, Hasegawa's stylised portraits become icons, symbols larger than language, replacing beings. Essence of Fan culture: The idea of Juliette Lewis is much more rewarding than she actually is.[23]

For Davies and Hasegawa, painting is a means of romanticising, internalising the virtual disorder. Concepts larger than life reduced to a symbol, manageable image-bites. Tangible, controlled, utilitarian. Idolised.

2.

I'm a man - I'm a goddess,
I'm a man - I'm a blue movie…[24]

On the cusp of the future, **Steven Gontarski** and **Gary Webb** project/design the better post-human. Genetically modified: nothing is sexier than intangible voyeurism.

Transhumanism: earthy brown techno abject love object. Gary Webb's automated cyborg sculpture gently rocks to it's churning rhythmic motor sound. In *God Knows* and *I Love Black Music* each component is individually manufactured: glass, metal, plastic. Frankensteinesses: Webb hobby-constructs his sci-fi beauties with heartfelt adoration. Unlike the usual portrayal of androids, Webb's creations are less scary than wondrous. As "TV landscapes"[25] they embody everything we've come to yearn. They are Grace-Jones-gorgeous. We are envious.

---

[21] Glam-god **David Bowie**, *Space Oddity*, <u>Changes</u>, 1975

[22] The sexy star of Eidos's ***Tomb Raider*** video games.

[23] The mere inkling of Juliette implores sordid promise of sultry-red-hot-white-trash-jail-bait. But the real Juliette Lewis lives in a tasteful New York apartment, does yoga and considered voting for Ross Perot.

[24] **Berlin**, *Sex (I'm A…)*, <u>Pleasure Victim</u>, 1982. …"I'm a virgin, I'm a slut, I'm a little girl…When we make love together…" Pre-***Top Gun*** when Berlin were still respectable.

[25] Artist's description: **Gary Webb** sits composed, rolling a cigarette, in his spacious studio apartment; A shock of blond hair sweeps across his forehead. Pausing reflectively, he takes a sip of his imported mineral water and contemplates, "They're TV landscapes, really."

Steven Gontarski's cyber-Classical sculptures are sexuality in the space age. Erotic biomorphic forms exude an onanistic wantonness: shiny plastic pleasure beings. Club-scene-latex-fashion: ultimate objects of desire posing and performing. Their seduction is only visible; they are self-fulfilling, as intangible as superstars. Gontarski's cover version of the *Dying Captive/Lying Active* has all the right mixtures of sensationalism. Paying homage to the world's sexiest sculpture, Gontarski also brings to light the contextualisation of Michelangelo as a 16th century society bad boy.[26] There is an historical entrenchment of art in the world of fashion; this is a renaissance of gossip.

Gontarski and Webb's sculptures celebrate sensation. Bordering between enticing and grotesque, the seduction lies in the passionate veneration of their making. This is more than mere infatuation, this is a love affair with the inanimate.

I.

There's a club if you'd like to go, you may meet somebody who really loves you,
so you go and you stand on your own, and you leave on your own
and you go home and you cry and you want to die[27]

Having it all and not knowing it. Martin Maloney and Shaun Roberts/Gilbert McCarragher deal with longing and loneliness in the fast lane. Endearingly superficial, fashionably desperate, the characters in these works anguish over the emptiness of being merely popular. This is a seduction in earnest.

Martin Maloney's paintings consummate the elements of single life as presented in the fashionable world of women's magazines.[28] His empathetic, always hopeful characters move through the clichéd circumstances of date fiction: Wearing the right clothes, making the right small talk, meeting that special someone. Striving for that When-Harry-Met-Sally kind of love, Maloney's paintings are tinged with futility, teenage impatience of perpetual lonely nights. Big screen emotion meets real-life rejection. Love is striking a pose, Tragedy is the inevitable morning after. Sedentary loneliness: attractive, desirable, addictive.

Teeth, Toes and Contact Lenses, Shaun Roberts/Gilbert McCarragher's teenage angst video captures all the elements of Trauma Style. Shot like a music video, the character is framed as the archetypal pin-up casualty. London-victim-glam-boy seeks all the attention: sulking for the sake of being sexy. Problems are all the rage, Bulimia a Diana-endorsed designer label. Power/manipulation: this boy's seduction lies in his infliction. His 'secret' trauma a performance for our arousal. Fucked up he needs us. We are completely romanced.

---

[26] Medici social-climbing, trans-sexualism in the Vatican, that bitchy Biagio de Cesena/Last Judgement scandal. Oh, if there were tabloids then!

[27] **The Smiths, *How Soon is Now*, Hatful of Hollow, 1984.**

[28] Conjure up images of self-conscious young women anxiously reading about how to spice up their relationship while they sit at home on Saturday night dreaming of the boyfriend they don't have. Although specifically a genre invented by women's magazines, it's now being adapted by other media as well i.e. TV's ***Ally McBeal,*** John Gray's mega-famous self-help sequel ***Mars and Venus On a Date.***

Freeze.

You've got the power to know.
You're indestructible[29]

Romantic Tragedy: The 20th century is an era of heroism. Everything is romanticised through media, packaged for desire. Millions of perfect images creating a perfect modern. For these artists Future Shock is obsolete. Emulating simulation, this generation cherish the Novocain hum of the synthetic. Fabricated woe is a youth anthem: Molly Ringwald,[30] My Own Private Idaho,[31] Moz.[32] Tragic heroes of indulgence and sensuality.

Die Young Stay Pretty surpasses the era of traditional heroism. Monumentous concepts such as luxury lifestyles, awe of nature, glamour of technology, adventure of future, fragility of love have all been ingrained into the realm of the video-normal. Yet there remains the passion for romance: these artists hand-craft, create, love and fantasize. The pleasure of making, being able to express a personal ideal of beauty, create their own perfection. Non-emotion larger than life; These artists are disclosing the utterly personal.

Achieving that feeling, monumental sentiment, the rush of the numb. This group revives the intimate, confides their seduction, and within the beauty, creates just a touch of empathetic, glamorous tragedy. In the thrust towards tomorrow, they are racing to immortalise the Now.

Die Young Stay Pretty.

---

[29] **Spandau Ballet,** *Gold,* *True*, **1983 ..."Gold. Always believe in your soul. You've got the power to know You're indestructibllllllllllllle, always believe in...."** There was some confusion about the lyrics because it's hard to tell if the background singers are saying **'to know'** or **'control'** or **'let's go'**, but Gontarski thinks it's **'to know'** and he's way cooler than I am so he must be right.

[30] Quintessential teenage star of ***The Breakfast Club, Sixteen Candles*** and ***Pretty in Pink.*** After having difficulty making the transition to grown up Hollywood roles Ringwald moved to France where she lived for 4 years. You do see her every now and again though in some made-for-TV stuff including Stephen King's epic saga ***The Stand*** and a movie-of-the-week about HIV. Rumour has it she is currently dating writer Valery Lameignere.

[31] Cult classic. Drugs, prostitution and Narcolepsy, loosely based on Shakespeare's Henrys. It's widely rumoured that this was the beginning of River Phoenix's flirtation with narcotics that lead to that fateful night at Johnny Depp's Viper Room.

[32] "Morrissey actively cultivated his self-made, anti-hero persona - the consummate Englishness, studied vulnerability, the awkward balance between exhibitionist and introvert, the self-proclaimed celibacy, and the quick and charming wit all combined to increase his notoriety and secure a more rabid fan base than ever before."
http://imusic.com/showcase/modern/morrissey.html

Gemma de Cruz in conversation with Martin Maloney, curator of Die Young Stay Pretty

30th September 1998

Lots of the artists in the show are relatively young. Do you think it has become easier for young artists to produce interesting new work and translate their ideas and concerns in relation to what's happening around them?

Well, first of all I don't think they are that young. I think that's a nice thing that you say....

Maybe young in the sense that they've just finished their MAs?

I think people want everything to be marketed as the cult of the young and the cult of the new, but look at their photographs and check the hair loss! There's a lot of them pushing thirty to forty. We're half way through our lives, but we're getting our first group show in a museum, and we're coming in on the breath of something new. Whatever we've been doing before, we have had different experiences to draw on. That's a cliché but I also think that it is quite true.

There are some young artists like Gary Webb?

Gary Webb, Caroline Warde, David Thorpe and Steven Gontarski. Jun's about thirty but she was successful straight out of college.

Do you think young artists are finding it easier to get their work shown, so they don't have to go through a bad patch after leaving college?

If you've made successful work in your degree show and you're in London, people will probably see it. If you haven't got a clear product, then it's more difficult. Art exists as a physical thing, it is the way in which people can see how your intelligence as an artist is manifested - via objects, or procedures. So if that clarity of thought doesn't come across in the work, then you've got a problem.

Starting to make art professionally is tough: you've got to manage a part-time job, try and work out whether you can afford a studio, then you've got to do a show somewhere, and often no one comes to see it, and you're bending over backwards even to get a mention in Time Out, and you start to think "Shall I give up?" or "Shall I persevere?". It's even harder if you left college ten years ago, and its taken you ten years to figure out what your work is, and how that's related to what's happening now. People leave college with a lot of information; they are talking about the latest shows, they're all going to private views, they're all reading Artforum magazine, they are constantly discussing whether an artist is any good or not. Recent graduates know what's going on. After ten years time, if you haven't been successful you might have lost contact with that intensity of debate.

So it's a danger that you might be locked into the ideas that were prevalent when you left college?

It would have been terrible to have fallen asleep in 1982 and woken up in 1998. London's a good place to be making work, especially now. Some people see Sensation as the end of something and they're looking for something new. Lots of people are saying "There's nothing out there" and other people want to herald any new artist as the latest thing. We are just trying to make our work and we're lucky to be in a receptive atmosphere. I am not saying "I am new" or "this is the end of an era". I can only say "I'm responding to art". Some things that are heralded as new become an embarrassment six months later.

I've learnt so much from looking at the work that's been done in the past ten years. But I didn't want my work to look like that. It had already been done, so what was the point of being the fifth person making Sarah Lucas type work when she makes it fine herself? If you are trying to open up the possibility of 'Non-ironic painting' and if the idea of narrative, or the idea of expression or of figuration, if that hasn't been done for ten years, or twenty years, then you're going to get a little bit more attention, because you've decided now is the time to do that. The fifth person who decides to do it gets a bit of attention. The twentieth person gets less, until somebody else decides something new. It's like Take That became the first boy band. They're not really the first boy band, but they were the first ones for a long time. And the Spice Girls became the first girl band.

After Bananarama!

Yes, but you're going to be more interested in the Spice Girls than you are in Bewitched. If you're saying "Now is the right time to be doing this, and here are some other people doing it" that gets some attention, just because you have the confidence to say it.

But isn't this work just a poor imitation of what has happened elsewhere?

The good thing for British Art is that artists can look at things around the world and they can make a British Art version, that is stridently international. The conservative streak of British art and British culture can be put to good use, and be a strength not a weakness. That is what makes it radical. It's not a culture that invents new art forms, it refines them. Something's invented in America and it's refined in England. The renewed interest in figuration didn't start in Britain, it happened in America. Karen Kilimnik, Elizabeth Peyton and John Currin and in some ways Mike Kelley, Jim Shaw and the LA school.

American art kicks the ball, and British artists grab it. Our version isn't like the American version. It isn't just a copy. It's like clothes, you grab your granny's dress, you chop the bottom off it, and you make it into something else. But really it's still your granny's dress. It's our sense of being receptive to traditional things infused with a punky rebellious spirit.

What does it mean to do this show now?

Just by being at the ICA says something. The ICA isn't neutral. They showed True Stories, which presented Karen Kilimnik and Jim Shaw for the first time in the UK, Bad Girls included Sue William's work. They did solo shows of Marlene Dumas, Luc Tuymans, and John Currin. They've had an active dialogue with important things. You don't bring important artwork over and then expect that just to be received by artists in a neutral way. When you bring new art in, if it makes sense among art students and emerging artists, it can cause an explosion. It opens up another seam of interesting things to mine, new avenues to explore. Museums who do shows are not neutral. So to put this show back in the ICA, made sense. I am placing this show back in the museum where some ideas were originally generated. There is a dialogue with that.

Is this a triumph for the DIY curator?

Maybe, I put a show on in my kitchen and my bedroom and my bathroom and in a couple of years time I was asked to do something at the ICA. I put on some shows and people responded.

What is your approach as a curator?

If you put ten things that seem to have a degree of similarity in terms of making, in terms of look, idea, what they are expressing, you are going to get something, whether a particular kind of look or kind of effect. I have in mind a particular mood for the show. I have chosen artworks which will work together and play off one another.

I'm not taking the works as just neutral things, I'm taking them as highly charged pieces which will work differently according to the context in which they are placed. I will allow the works to 'speak' individually, but how they are hung in relation to each other is also crucial. I'm not interested in an '80s thing of the neutrality of the museum space. The key to the show is the mood. It's a ghost train. A house of fun. I want people to experience the show as one whole thing. I want them to feel something at the end - something which will be generated by how the show has been arranged. I want it to be theatrical, but without the trivial connotations of that.

I think of the show like making a film. Picking the works is like casting the actors, and I am the director. I am choosing how to light it, and I've got the script.

Maybe seeing fifty artists in one show is not going to give the impact.

No. That would be like pick and mix. Too much like a survey show.

How did you choose the artists?

I was thinking "who does this the best", and so that made the selection very easy. I've been watching people for a while. Thinking "Was it a gimmick? Was it a one-off? Are they a serious artist?". When you do a show that's what you are saying "These are the ones I think are important", and you need a little bit of inside information to do that. You can't always judge it on seeing an object. But that's what other people have to judge it on. They see a piece of sculpture for example, and think "This is good, this is a good artist". So it will be interesting in terms of what happens afterwards to see who's still there in two years, if people do want artistic careers, and who disappears.
I made a list of about fifty or sixty people whose work interested me and who were doing new kinds of things with traditional forms or subjects. I knew some of the artists from teaching, from seeing other shows. I have discovered some work in degree shows, there are all sorts of ways that things

get drawn to my attention. There are hundreds of artists doing similar kinds of work. I then went through the list and thought whose work do I really like? and took some people off the list. Whose work still seemed new? There were certain people who I might have had on, but I thought "They've been around for a while, and it seems they haven't had a context, but they do have a context just because they've been in the public eye for a while.". I think I am showing the artists who are doing their best work now. I've already worked with some of the artists at Lost in Space - (the gallery I ran in my Brixton flat) because I thought their work was still interesting.

So you already know what the work of the Lost In Space artists looks like together.

Yes, but people's work changes. I think it was about who was going to be a serious artist, and who was going to take the opportunity seriously, and who I knew would, at the end of the day, make the work and deliver the goods. I am taking a risk on people. Some artists have known, proven track records and some artists don't.

I just thought, what would make an interesting group, or interesting pairings? So there was the good version of something, the bad version of something else, the scary version, the pretty version, something that needed to be twenty foot long, something that needed to be twelve inches tall, I was thinking about formal things, and how the works would play off each other. Sculpture was important because there was a lot of new sculpture being made, but although I knew lots of people doing photography I couldn't find anyone who would fit in.

And video?

In Lost In Space shows I always had drawing and wall drawing and painting and objects and installation pieces. They were materially very eclectic. This show is probably less eclectic, there is more painting than anything else. There's only one filmmaker in the show. I suppose I was looking for work that I wasn't going to be bored by, and didn't seem pretentious. With Shaun Roberts's films, I'd liked them and I'd shown them before, they are rather like films that you could watch on TV. They seemed like fun. I didn't want a twenty-foot projection, because that seemed very 1993. I wanted something that had a narrative, and was dreamy and romantic. There's a certain look that I liked. With a lot of videos you feel it must be doing you good somewhere along the line, but it isn't interesting. I didn't want a high-tech show either, and I didn't want something that was too documentary.

How do you fit yourself in it? It must be hard to be making decisions about people's work, and at the same time remembering that your work is going to be in the show as well?

Either you put yourself in the show or you don't. I always put myself in the Lost In Space shows, and at the beginning my work wasn't really as good as the people I was curating, because I hadn't really worked out how to do it. By the time Die Yuppie Scum happened at Karsten Schubert my work had improved and now I have worked out how to do it. I have been offered shows, I am more focused.

It's a strange thing being a curator, because you're doing something to do with taste, and something to do with intellectual choice, something to do with bringing new things to people's attention, something to do with stamping your seal of approval and saying "Martin Maloney thinks these artists have interesting work or are talented".

What about the title? It could mean so many things.

What do you think it could mean?

Well, it's like The Rolling Stones can mean 'Rolling Stones' as in rock 'n' roll, it can mean "a rolling stone gathers no moss", rolling stones as in 'stoned'. It's like that. And Die Young Stay Pretty, can mean "die" as in serious, "pretty" as in not serious. To me, it's like my worst fear is to die, and the only thing I want is to stay pretty. It's getting a bit metaphorical, but I think a lot of the work is like that. It's about having the balance of something that's got a lot of energy, but looks really simple. That has a lot of knowledge, but looks easy. You can take the title as saying "These are the cool kids". How do you interpret it?

I've always had titles that I thought were fun. I think there's nothing more boring than 'twelve new artists'. I'm putting forward a title that will attract an audience because they're intrigued by what it means. I don't think you can completely decipher it, and it's not exactly a narrative. It's a mood setter. It involves a play with language: when I did Die Yuppie Scum, that was a very aggressive title for what was actually quite a sweet show. I suppose it addressed Karsten, who was the archetypal yuppie. At the ICA I'm directly addressing my audience with this title. I'm saying "This is you". You are these people in black polo-neck jumpers, who are too thin to be true. You are living one of these beautiful lives. You are butterflies. You are different people from when I first came here fifteen years ago, and yet you are the same. And you will be coming here in ten years time. Generally there's a play on James Dean, River Phoenix and Marilyn Monroe. The title implies glamour and nihilism which I really like - it's romantic, it's about Hollywood and T.V. It says "just live for today". It can also be broken down into four individual words on their own. You can imagine it said with a Bruce Nauman robotic sounding voice so that it doesn't become a phrase: DIE / YOUNG / STAY / PRETTY. The title plays with what people want to be. They want to be young, they want to be beautiful, they want to be those things forever. And the only way you can be those things forever is if you make the ultimate sacrifice. Of course you don't really want to die, but you do probably want to watch your own funeral. That would be the big thrill wouldn't it. To see that people really cared and were upset. But then that's a very shallow thing to want; I'm playing with shallowness.

But what do you think the show says beyond the title?

The show is a discussion about beauty, about decoration and how those aesthetic ideas are mediated through t.v. culture. Much of the work suggests a pleasure in making and looking at art. Craft skills are embraced but they are not used as craft but as art. There is a lot of cutting and sewing. Intellectually it's collage but it doesn't look like fragmentation. Fragile materials and simple methods are used in gentle but assertive ways. Who would have thought that paper cut outs could be used as a radical art material?

But it's not just methods and materials, traditional subjects are used too.

The imagery of landscape, still life, the interior, the figure, animals are all included but not in a pure way. Pop art changed that. It's realism became a standard for the late twentieth century. The graphic qualities of illustrated, flat or cartoon imagery, have been used as a source for their graphic clarity. But this is not a revival of Pop art, which was very mechnically made and obviously concerned with found commercial sources. What is more noticeable is that the insistence on realism through the photographic or documentary has slipped from view.

There is a distinct lack of irony in the work

The works put forward a direct and immediate relationship with artistic expression and the imagination. I see a strong expressive quality in the work without that falling into the pitfalls of re-working a crazed expressionism.

So no one is airing their dirty laundry in public?

The artists do share a belief in making the ordinary dramatic rather than shocking. Anger has been soothed - no one wants to rip anyone's head off. It's art with a smile rather than a snarl. Any horror is low key, shown more as a moody brooding than blood, guts and gore. The work looks romantic in a bored day-dreamy way. It's like looking out of the window and wanting something nice to happen.

So this is not the Romantic sublime?

The dreamy qualities in the artworks do not express a personal poetic. They come from the commercial exploitation of our desire for that poetic. The artworks show the blank beauty of a generation seduced by the romantic poses of people, places and things from t.v. and magazines. Narcissism is strong in much of the work, without the artists using images of themselves or adopting a 'me, me, me' confessional stance. The legacy of club culture echos in much of the work. There is a shared fantasy of "Be who you want to be. See only what you want to see.". When I look at the work I feel shocked by the artists' fascination with the trivial. I see the emptiness of the superficial but somehow I've been made to enjoy that.

David Thorpe

Friday 18th September

the word "kitsch" annoys me. I think kitsch is when you take high culture and bring it low.

But I think I'm doing the reverse.

I'm taking familiar images and giving them strength.

I don't feel I'm a painter.

I never really sat down and thought I will do landscape.

I almost can't think of any other subject particularly to do.

I came out of doing photographs and photo collages. And then it was a way of mixing together an interest of photography and film. It was a method of incorporating all my interests without it being tied to any one of them.

Its only as they've got bigger have I realised the link with these to the landscape tradition within painting of liking and starting to look again at Claude, Friedrich and Fragonard particularly. It was almost once I was into it that I realised I was actually doing "landscape". Initially I was making pictures of buildings and night-time. Mainly because, walking around at twilight things becomes mysterious and interesting. It was important because of the silhouettes that nothing was too specific. Initially they started off with these figures and they've got less and less important.

The silhouette adds an ambiguity to the whole thing. Also I think its more romantic. Daylight. Everything's too bright, too clear, too visible. This is like a mystery.

I don't see a huge amount of difference between looking at certain Fragonards and certain Alex Katz, even though there might be three hundred years or whatever between them. Katz is one of the few painters to show a great beauty in his work. Its about fashion and lifestyle.

They were actually quite simple. Also at one stage I wasn't sure whether to go slightly simpler or more detailed. I think because I saw them and they were quite simple I thought I'd go the other way and make them more detailed.

I don't have any interest in painting. I think if I directly translated these to paintings just as flat areas of colour they'd be so uninteresting. I think there's a domination in painting as the serious art form and you're not really serious unless you're painting. I think it would be very difficult to paint a lot of these scenes. They'd relate too close to Friedrich, or become kitsch or too clichéd. So it is a nice way to (hopefully) still be able to do pictures that maybe in painting it would be difficult to do.

I see the New Cross/ London Bridge area and then go back and try to make them even better.

When I started I wanted to do something that was very intricate, very delicate, very humble, modest, but at the same time the subject matter might be quite grand and quite big. Bold. Initially it was about the jet set lifestyle so I was using very humble, fragile low key materials against these modernist jet set scenes. Even though it's less jet set and more urban, the subject matter seems to be about elements of modernism and the technique seems more craft based. Low key, hands on and I think that balance works quite well.

subject matter seemed to be about alienation and urban space and can seem bleak. But these are joyous and have excitement to the world. A lot of modernist

I'm happy for people to see how they're made. How they're stuck down and what the source is. That its art-shop paper. Sometimes you can see pencil marks from the stencils. I don't want to be too perfect even though there's a temptation to get intricate in the way the work is finished. I don't want it to be too pristine or look like something done on computer.

The technique is modestly romantic as well. Flat painted paintings don't really give off anything in terms of emotion. Its about anonymity. You're continually aware of the flatness.

I can essentially make fairly traditional pictures and it still seems very new. When people realised how to do depth and linear perspective. There must've been a joy to the whole thing. I wanted that and this is a physical way of making pictures.

looking at that and re-enjoying these scenes. I think the technique allows the audience to start

I'm a big Raymond Carver fan and I think that helped the initial subject matter. His stuff was about insubstantial narrative. It was OK to make pictures of two people sitting on a balcony looking at the sky. Nothing big has to happen. Its almost like nothings going on in the narrative, but then there's a lot going on.

The illusion could fall apart at any minute. you're always aware of how flat it is.

The primary interest was in a way of making pictures again. I think I then tried to work out a way which even though the images are familiar in film stills, and seem familiar, the techniques employed are very personal. That seems very important as a way to get intimate with the subject matter again. Even though I'm using familiar cultural scenes, I'm still making them my own.

Interviewed by Gemma de Cruz

left:
David Thorpe, Dare to Thrill, 1998
paper, 60 x 65cm, courtesy the artist

above:
David Thorpe, Ready to Burn, 1998
paper, 165 x 160cm, courtesy the artist

Jun Hasegawa
24th September 1998

my work has a relationship with space and architecture.

I can't make abstract things.

It's been cut-out from the start.

Sometimes I think I want to say something through my work, emotional things. I thought that about the explosion. I wanted to say something about feeling angry. I wanted to put a fire on somebody's car. I learnt quite a lot from making an explosion just to show an emotional feeling. Before, my girls didn't have any emotional feeling. They looked very cold, but now I try to give my people emotions.

I think part of my work is a mixture of so many different categories. It's painting, but it's got 3D elements and installation as well. I hang them quite a bit away from the wall and sometimes stand them up from the floor. It's always something to do with space. It's not like a painting hung on the wall.

Sometimes I get confused whether my work is painting or sculpture.

I just chose beautiful people. And also, I like the artificiality of film and actors and actresses. I think it's appropriate to my work. I'm trying to create my fantasy world in a gallery space. If you think of this material, MDF and gloss paint, they're artificial materials, casual as well. You can get them from a DIY shop. There's a glossy image and surface which I highlight as well. I'm adding something.

When I see the picture I just see the face. I don't see the back of them. I take the surface, the shadows. I transform from the photograph.

I don't see my work as a cartoon. I see it as a graphic image. I like the idea of creating a fantasy world that everyone can watch. It's different from realistic drama.

To me it doesn't really matter who they are. I do sometimes make it models. Now I have famous people or sometimes friends, but I always work from a photograph, a flat picture of real people, so even though they're famous, or friends, the process of making is the same. Also, I see it more as an abstract image in my work, like a flat colour, simple lines and shadows. If the colours match each other I'm quite happy with that. I don't see them as "famous".

Paul Weller in the 70's was still quite stylish. He's wearing a Fred Perry shirt and even his watch is stylish. He's got a cool image.

Paul Weller. I don't think he could wear bright red polo shirts.

I try not to choose "portraits". Sometimes in a film the actor is sitting in front of a camera but he's talking to somebody else.

I change the colours quite a lot sometimes. I put creases in the clothes. I look at the colour of her skin and then maybe the objects ie. the telephone. Then I think about the colour of the clothes. She's got red lips and blue eyes so I gave her green clothes. I wouldn't give her orange because it's too reddish. When I start painting I'm not thinking of them as famous people or who they are. I just see a graphic image and matching colours. Leonardo is wearing a T-shirt and polo shirt, in the middle you can just see a tiny print on his T-shirt So I see three colours and how I can paint them. Then I concentrate on those three colours. I've got ten different colour charts just of Leonardo.

Matching colours is very important.

I'm learning every day. I think I try to match colours to their feelings and personality. I think the people are as they are but I add something by the colours I use. Simplifying the lines or using shadows. Probably I see them as icons too. I haven't changed anything. I think there is a difference between the famous people and the people I know. I change the friends a lot. Try to make my own things. With the famous people I'll just follow the lines.

I'm interested in **Ellsworth** Kelly's painting. I think because he works with different shaped canvases on a space. Maybe I have a similar idea of using architecture of a space and colour. Also, when I went to the show at the Tate Gallery I felt like I was going to a temple. I had a very good feeling. I also like a lot of American artists. Pop artist - Andy Warhol, Roy Lichtenstein, Alex Katz.

Lisa Milroy, Richter **Alessandro Raho.** They're far from reality even though they all paint from reality.

Charles Ray. He makes quite realistic sculpture of people but they're quite empty. I like that.

I like to show my work. It's to do with confidence too. When I make something nice, big, beautiful, it gives me confidence to continue. I think if I was making tiny, small work it wouldn't really give me that confidence. That's important.

Also cut-outs are different to photographs. Making it is important. The craft, and how the hand made it. If I took a photograph and showed it in a gallery it would feel too easy. I want to be involved and make my own things that no-one else can make. That's why I didn't choose to work in oil on canvas. I think I would do a realistic painting like Lisa does, but I don't want to.

This show is about enjoying making work and how it's made. It's very important to me. **I spent a long** time making the work and it makes me excited to get new ideas. Although the format is the same; cut-outs, simple, flat colour and line, the subject matter has changed from fashion models to actors, to friends. I always change the subject matter.

As I said, I'm quite shy and don't really talk to people. So when I work I make my own fantasy world.

Interviewed by Gemma de Cruz

above:

Jun Hasegawa, Orange, Blue and Yellow, 1998

gloss paint on MDF, 250 x 150 x 17cm, courtesy the artist

right:

Jun Hasegawa, Juliette Lewis, 1998

gloss paint on MDF, 122 x 110 x 17cm, courtesy the artist

Dexter Dalwood
4th September 1998

I am not interested in painting personal paintings from memory,

It's to do with confidence and thinking I'll just try it and if i make a fool of myself it doesn't really matter. If you've been looking and thinking about whats happened in painting.

I would like people to see this painting and think "oh wow I could paint that - you mean its alright to paint those things"

I know that theres going to be other people would absolutely hate these paintings and find them kitsch or whatever I like very minimal painting and I like exuberant painting. I like all sorts of painting so you know I just think its the idea that there's room to exist in. It seems what happened in all that debate when you talk about the beginning of the nineties, suddenly everything felt a bit airless. If you weren't somehow doing something to do with Richter or something which was about the debate between photography and painting then you were kind of not doing something serious. And I think thats a shame because when you go back to when I was at art school if you said to someone then that you liked Gustav Klimt they would have giggled and said who do you really like. ie a serious painter. But it seems to me why can't it be that I really like Munch, but I don't want to paint things that look like those paintings, so I'm talking about painting in terms of the spirit of them in 1998. Cezanne on the one level he appeals to everyone, if you dont know anything about painting, you see a beautiful landscape,If you're a painter you start thinking these are so complicated. So intelligently made, so risky, so anarchic.

using bits of found photographs (never of the actual places) from design magazines, hello magazines, and from the description of the actual places.

places that I haven't physically seen or haven't actually physically been to.

it is a fictional place of some sort.

What I then do is I start doing pencil drawings to get a physical idea of the space and where I want to be. So I can be looking at it from a certain angle
And then I try to find things that vaguely fit into the perspective. I've got to try & find a bed that goes from left to right & if I can't find one I'll make one out of two or three put together.

when you first see it,
could be a real place, but then you realise things are slightly wonky.
So as you start to look at it doesn't add up.

if you think of someone like Jeff Wall, what he does is the idea that when you first look at some of his images they are very convincing, the more you look at them you realise they're not. But for me the idea of the photograph is not so interesting, for me its like, painting becomes more intimate than the realism of photographs. And then what happens, when I make the collages, part of the excitement of making the painting is looking at things and

thinking how am I going to paint that. How am I physically going to paint something that I cut out, am I going to spray it on? There's the excitement of invention about it. And then thinking about other artists, and the relationship to that is very important. When I did that Laboratoire Garnier I was thinking about Mondrian and I was thinking about Klimt. The idea of Mondrian/Klimt type painting in 1998 which didn't look like either of those artists but had the sort of feeling of that order, romance, and glitz at the same time.

There are also other references like in the Liberace painting I was thinking of the Hollywood film maker Douglas Sirk - did very romantic interiors very lavish and over the top. Also photographers, the American Walker Evans he did all these very amazing photos of places, interiors and exteriors. I am interested in 17th century dutch interior painting through to american photography, Mondrian, Munch, Klimt, Kippenburger, Philip Guston and Martin Scorsese - the whole thing and everything else in life. Its really an idea like why can't you put together everything you really like & make a painting from it. The difference is, early in the decade, the relationship of the different things - if something was going to be postmodern it had to show it was coming from different places. In a David Salle painting he had photo images with cartoon images - nothing is more important than everything else. Now I think its possible to forget about that and amalgamate it all, because it's accepted. Why wouldn't you be able to use all those different ways of painting for making images again, which are images of the real things but they're not because they're fantasy places.

in fantasy, and how that idea of fantasy can exist and you can exist in the fantasy space. And then the subjective part for me is that they are places that I would like to go to and can almost see myself going to.

its alright to be slightly obsessional if it is what you're really interested in

I think there are a lot of cul-de-sacs in painting and the

trouble with saying that is that it sets up a binary argument

- one thing is good and another thing is bad.

For me Philip Guston is a big influence, but not how he physically painted or how his paintings look. But how he talked about his painting and the ideas he had. The thing is that he always said that when he left the studio at night he left a world behind. He wasn't leaving "was the red working next to the green" he was leaving a world of some sort that's something I'm very interested in. When I get up in the night & think about these places which exist.

Time is a strange thing.
You work things through. Its strange how I can see familiar ideas
They don't look like the paintings I did before but its the things underneath it I've always been interested in You could say that what I've always been interested in is painting something which isn't actually there. Depicting something which can't actually be seen and also things poking through and being juxtapositioned which add up to make a strange combination. Now its all homogenised into one thing.

big themes. I don't feel you have to be hard hitting in your face in the same way. I think theres a lot of sex & death in these but in a different way which. I think there is kitsch & romance in a different kind of way.

Its like the excitement of being in the cab on your way to the party so its all ahead, its before you get there you're on the guest list or something youre gonna get in its the buzz you get. I'd love to convey that in a painting.

Interviewed by Gemma de Cruz

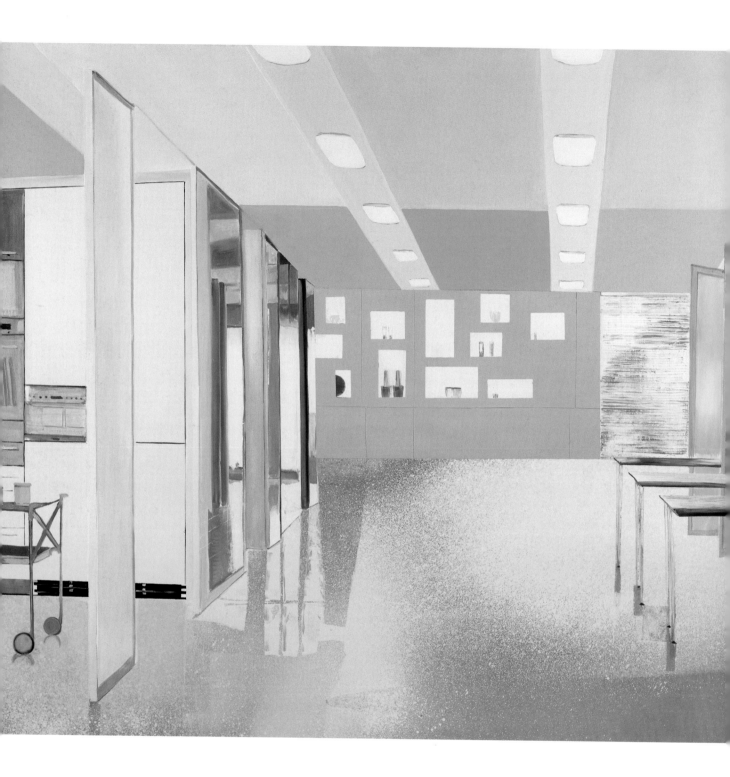

Dexter Dalwood, Laboratoire Garnier, 1998
oil on canvas, 183 x 235cm, courtesy the artist

Dexter Dalwood, Paisley Park, 1998
oil on canvas, 153 x 183cm, collection Saatchi Gallery, London

Peter Davies
23rd September 1998

Interviewed by Gemma de Cruz

For a long time the generation before us got all the attention. Maybe it's because our work wasn't good enough. things have changed so much in the last six months in relation to what is seen as *our generation* of artists who a year ago no one gave a shit about.

I realised it looked different but it's all the same.

"Die Yuppie Scum" I did two paintings and they were both different; one was text and one was abstract. So there was this relationship between the two which was important to me.

Although I think you can make quite clear distinctions between figurative and abstract I think they're kind of irrelevant as definitions any more any more and they're not things I really think about because I don't need to.

Both the abstract and text painting would be on a white background, there'd be lots of different colours and randomly organised. The way in which I made and filled in the painting was very similar, except the text painting had words. What surprised me was the way in which people reacted to the text painting. I always thought that having a lot to read was asking too much of the viewer but its surprising that people actually quite like it and it makes it easier for them because they don't have to really think.

So I became aware that to improve the abstract paintings you had to have as much a sense of content in a literal way as you had in the text paintings.
In the beginning one of the interests for me doing it was that I had all this interest in art history which was great and exciting but quite intimidating as well, trying to find a way to make a painting and then include all that stuff in it. It's quite a tall order. More recently what I wanted to do was make the abstract paintings contain all that information i.e. what I like and don't like, what I know and don't know, what's good or bad. But from my own point of view.

I have a lot more ideas for abstract paintings than I do for the text paintings. I feel with the text painting I have to be more careful. You're really putting yourself on the line in a way because you're saying things quite directly so everything that seems laid back about them has to be measured and manipulated. So something that seems just funny is funny enough, it's not too funny, stupid, but not too stupid.

Maybe I'm being slightly simplistic,

read it now and think I can't believe I said that.

Process painting is pretty

quick and pretty flashy.

You can get amazing results

but intellectually it's very

boring.

my work

was a reaction against it

but also another way of

doing it.

how I go about making a painting it's always kind of the same for me. There's no radical
change of idea.

I just get these moods and think I'm just gonna tell them what I fucking think and then I get really excited because then that allows me the opportunity to say what I want rather than what I think I should say. That's when it really comes together. I say what I want but within reason. If you say fuck this and fuck that It'd be so boring.

Richard Prince   I could   relate to his attitude

The ones you read ("Art I Like"...)
Everyone compared them to Sean Lander's painting which pissed me off. They're very pretty but didn't have high visual impact and I wanted to work out a way to do something snappy and aggressive and slightly more to the point. Doing the "Top 100" fulfilled that in a way. I was worried people wouldn't like them because they didn't have the funny comments. ...they were more difficult because of all the anxiety in trying to work out where the people went in the chart.

It's not so ordered in a way because there's an element of kow towing to prevalent wisdom and an element of putting two fingers up to all that. So it varies throughout the piece enormously. It does with all the text pieces. With "Art I Like" pieces, you get some silly thing I thought up about the artist or something someone's said or I've read. Sometimes it's accidental. My favourite is "I heard a thud it was Donald Judd" because it's so totally moronic. But also I can imagine him smashing his way into your house in a fury because you wrote a bad review about him.

With the charts, I feel that I am negotiating with something. I think right, this person is going here because I really like them and I think they're important and up yours to anyone who doesn't.

In a way my attitude to the work has changed as well. When I first did the text painting I was feeling pretty angry about various things and I feel angry now but about different things.

Wanting to be on the same page as all these artists but the only way I could do it was by putting them all in my painting. Now, sometimes I think some of the humour is quite juvenile, which I think is quite nice.

There are great things about all sorts of different artists. Like Gainsborough or whoever. If you approach it from too learned an attitude you miss out on the reality, so the way in which things are drawn in to culture nowadays are so quick. It's not meaningless because the meaning in things is so hyper-fast and sophisticated that people are able to understand much more quickly than they've ever been before so you can take Gainsborough and say "he's cool because he's the original bad painter" rather than saying "Gainsborough is very interesting to the history of British art because of blah blah blah" because you think well who gives a shit. It's like every five minutes Art can be this exciting thing you can relate to your present world. It's much, much better, even if that's quite a trashy way of dealing with it than him being some boring, dead old guy.

I just think if you look at the way fashion is always trying to plunder things that aren't fashionable to make them fashionable like styles from previous eras. When 70's retro fashion first came in, it seemed so horrible it couldn't be fashionable. But now it's so acceptable it doesn't seem at all radical or weird. That's the way the world operates now.

constant sense of what you're actually doing and a sort of ambiguity in relation to the   So you have to maintain a meanings people place on it out of your control.

So if my painting just looked like decorative pattern, that could be interesting for five minutes, but then, who cares? It's got to look like not just op art, but op art and twenty different other things at the same time.

overleaf left: Peter Davies, *Study for Coloured Painting*, 1998
acrylic on canvas, 35.6 x 48.9cm, courtesy the artist

overleaf right: Peter Davies, *Study for Black Squares and White Squares in Squares Painting*, 1998
acrylic on canvas, 35.6 x 48.9cm, courtesy the artist

I seem able to talk about the work when I'm talking about the same things over and over again but you do come up to all these little stumps when you're making completely different things.
I'm dealing with different work in different ways.

I think they're probably all about the same thing but the trickiness is finding what the thing is that is going on, that makes them want to be made.

it's great fun making the stuff and working.

Some of it comes from drawing,

one was invented as it was made and then worked through.

"I Love Black Music", and "White City" they're straight forward analogies of what characters they are. This one ("I love black music") moves as well, The sound just comes from the motor churning around.

It's not about 70's furniture.
I think that there was a bit of furniture in the beginning but that faded away and I moved towards something else. I maybe drifted into it and then drifted away from it. It was a learning process. Making an object that size (White City) isn't something I've done before it was a lot smaller. I'm starting to feel comfortable working with that size, it's also a better size to be dealing with when you're changing stuff.

There is something quite pretend about making something really clean that underneath is a bit shabby. In the way it slots together and is glued, not quite up to manufacturing quality. They've got that glossy feel but the details close up reveal that it has been hand made and then they lose that shine.

('I Love Black Music') I wanted her to dance.

I brought down to a very basic way that would resemble someone dancing.

the skills that I have, they are also skills that I'm working on; how well materials go together.
I don't think they are figurative. The heads are part of the abstractness of them. They don't seem to be doing a great deal they're just connected to the other parts.
Other people make some of the parts but I put it all together. I put bits and pieces together but its difficult when you're making something to do it all yourself. A lot is missing from that presence of not doing all of it yourself but a lot is gained. You can get a straight down the line shape that first came to you.
It still works out to be the same it doesn't matter who ends up making it. Its the real tightness and order of knowing exactly what you want to make . So it ends up looking like you made it

There are things about the work that can be pushed in to groups . This group of work, that group of work, then there are three or four different types of groups that will end up over a period of time being really quite interesting as seperate groups, it just takes a long time to get to it. It's just beginning now so so it's hard to see . Somewhere the work will start comming together very stongly.
You can sit
for hours making up little stories about the way they feel and how they all connect to eachother. But God knows whether they do.

There does seem something endless about other people describing the work.

Interviewed by Gemma de Cruz

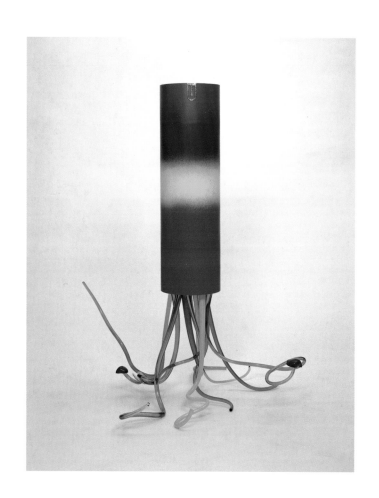

left:

Gary Webb, God Knows, 1998

perspex cylinder, glass, plastic fruit, paper and acrylic paint
160 x 125cm, collection Frank Cohen

above:

Gary Webb, I Love Black Music, 1998

aluminium, perspex, latex, gold thread, paint and electrical motor,
100 x 60cm, courtesy the artist and The Approach, London

Shaun Roberts with Gilbert McCarragher
28th September 1998

Bulimia isn't the crux of the film.

It's going to be an artistic film

This is why we want

it to be seductive and

beautiful even the

way he vomits.

He's very insecure.

he's in the privacy of his house.

It's his control thing.

He wants to live his life

in soft focus and live as if

he's in a magazine.

S : MTV has really promoted the idea of " You've got to be a wild party animal or you're not alive ". Everybody thinks that everybody's having a better time than them

men are under pressure to look a certain way. especially gay men,

Its becoming quite ridiculous, the whole thing. Its making a lot of people very unhappy.

We thought its becoming a bit obscene. out on the scene,

With gay men, you are your own object of desire.

There's a narcissistic feedback all the time. They're trying to look for love, but it's in a looking-glass world.

GM : The idea for the film came from somebody saying to me " I learned how to become bulimic from watching *Oprah* "

GM : This character is the sort of person who would ring up the Samaritans and pretend to be something that he's not. Perhaps he's not even bulimic - he just wants to be a part of the Rikki Lake thing. Its not just that he's bulimic, he's got a personality disorder. If he wasn't bulimic he'd be something else.

S : Gilbert's stronger on the narrative.

we want to put across is that the film doesn't have a logical narrative which is going to be resolved. Very often personality disorders are never resolved, it gets worse and becomes bizarre.

GM : We went through the story-boards together.   GM : The idea for it came from people I know.

We feel that it has to look like shimmery surface glamour and show how ethereal and superficial it is. Super-realist painting is everything but. We want music that takes it into popular music, we don't want it to be morose. Its going to change - start disco-ey then change.

You either get a narrative, or an aesthetic with no story. So its weaving the whole thing together. Stuff I've done before always starts with the soundtrack.

S : I think a lot of video Art is made because it's video And they've got an idea of what video Art should look like. We've got something to say and were saying it basically. A lot of video Art involves repetition and is used like a canvas I think a lot of people are turned off by that and it ends up being really pretentious. Most of it turns me off. A lot of video Art can be said in different ways, people often use it because it is a modern medium, it tends to be used in a conceptual way and I don't think it's always the best medium for that.

We were looking through some magazines and you could not take the gay press

seriously. You wonder how you're supposed to behave.

we do get obsessed by going to clubs and getting dressed up. Its

normally a phase and you grow out of it but some people don't.

Take drug culture, how many times do you go to a club and find people all off there face on an E dancing away; no ones communicating. No ones having a party with other people their having an individual good time on their own, in the club, but why go out to do that?

Interviewed by Gemma de Cruz

above:
Shaun Roberts and Gilbert McCarragher,
Teeth, Toes and Contact Lenses, 1998
u-matic video, courtesy the artists

right:
Shaun Roberts and Gilbert McCarragher,
Teeth, Toes and Contact Lenses, 1998
u-matic video, courtesy the artists

People always ask why I use these blue, greyish colours but Life is quite grey, London especially.

Working with thread is something that's become my technique. Using it is sometimes quite elaborate so slowly I'm building with it, especially if I use the example of the houses literally I'm building the house stone by stone, step by step, by the use of thread. I think of it like building that memory from the recollection of influences from the past, in the present, maybe even building the future.

I think if I had embroidered the whole image then I would go too far, it would really be too much like craft or folk art. I use both, the thread & the paint and I can think a couple of steps ahead when I make the painting I can make this red or that pink. It's also important when you have the image that there are certain details which are more important so they deserve more work, and more detail. Others are empty. There are things happening on the surface of the overall image which hopefully make your eye float around the image.

I'm working with landscape I'm dealing more with perspective. And you find out rules within the painting making a rock big because it's in front, make it small to suggest that rock is far away. Otherwise I can think certain details are important but the viewer may look at details that are important to them.

I always try to find different means for how to use thread. How to give the tree volume, it seems a logical way. They look do look dark and quite sad. If you stand between a couple of trees it doesn't have to be a forest, it can be very spooky.

I know these trees can look spooky so then I might put a flowery plant in front of it to get it more in balance.

They look traditional in the subject matter, the genre is landscape painting. When I was in Holland people thought that my paintings looked American.

Sometimes I copy a photographic image onto paper then from the paper I go to the canvas and don't look at the photo any more.

When I make a house I need straight lines you put the thread through one point & out another and it creates a straight line.
If you make a bush you want it to be fluffy so you use a certain type of wool.

A house can be a fantastic place but you don't know from the outside what's happening inside. I think it depends on the viewer. I manipulate it but the viewer decides.

I don't fill everything in I leave room for the viewer to step into the image.

We've seen so many images that we can finish it ourselves, we have a collective memory.

Fashion is able

to give the first signs

of what's happening now.

Clothes are the first

way for a person to have

identity.

Interviewed by Gemma de Cruz

above:

Michael Raedecker, haze, 1998

acrylic and thread on linen, 137.2 x 177.8cm,

courtesy the artist and The Approach, London

right:

Michael Raedecker, spot, 1998

oil, acrylic and thread on linen, 157.5 x 203.2cm,

courtesy the artist and The Approach, London

My work is more Disney reject

The kind of animals that appear through the history of painting are the ones I'm interested in making.

I had been making animals, which had nothing to do with animals.

animals suggest something about a human condition or human

relationships being represented through the animals.

animals have been used throughout Art History to make some comment about what was happening at

different times in different circumstances.

In the past, I've made sculpture which is an animal on a base, or a box or next to a tree, now I've decided to isolate those things, I still think that the tree can look slightly animal like, but I wanted to give it a go. It goes back to the idea of the still life, animals are normally in a scenario whether they are in a forest or standing next to a person it is all very staged. I wanted to see if I could get that kind of relationship between the objects and the animals.

The animal can become part of the tree stump or vice versa.

some people thought they looked like they were dead.

Some people thought that they looked like livers, or human organs

Or people say they look like garden ornaments and porcelain figurines, something that

blends in to its surroundings.

I wanted all of those connotations really. There is an intention

I started using clay to make the animals and a lot of people said to me that it was a strange thing to be doing, very old fashioned and a bit peculiar. Then, when they were cast and sprayed they liked it because they saw the twist. At Goldsmiths I hadn't really been around people that made sculpture in a traditional way the only person in my year who was close was Jun and her work wasn't necessarily sculpture. That's why I thought I'd do an M.A. where I could concentrate on traditional sculpture but it had the reverse effect. It became very isolating because they said I wasn't doing it properly, when I said what do you mean properly they said "well you don't mould clay like that". What I discovered was that I'd found a way of moulding clay through knowing nothing about it, but it became more interesting. If I had been more technically able the work would never have turned out the way it has,

I think if anyone who knew the correct, technical way of making the work saw me doing it they'd try and shoot me.

I think If I did make the work in a very technical way it wouldn't be so interesting.

It is like seeing something sad in a cartoon

I want it to reflect a moment when something sad happens, Often people can't show any emotion and the only emotion they can show is to laugh. It's a nervous thing in a way, when you can't quite believe something you laugh. I wanted them to be caught between that point.

I want it to be quite amusing but no one ever gets that.

I like the way painting. In hunting scenes you would have the animals from the wild that had been slayed by the hunter, then you would have the domestic animals like a cat looking round from the corner of the picture. What Im trying to say is that it's not that one thing is passive and one thing is aggressive; it's not true you are both things.
They all have potential to survive or not survive, to be sinister or not to be.

There is a similar sense of giving the animals a character of their own, in the Disney films the characters are given the identity of a human being. I don't watch that much Disney I've never seen Bambi. I love Watership Down that would be more interesting to me, rabbits with one eye and a chewed ear.

I got a review from Brian Sewell and he said the only memorable thing about my horses was that they looked like rejects from 'The Godfather' and that's exactly what I would like people to think. There are lots of things that make up what you are interested in but that's one scene I always think of in relation to that film.

A lot of it is left up to chance, If the clay becomes heavy and moves, then I go with the way it moves. It sounds quite hideous, for example I started making a deer for the ICA which had huge antlers pulling its head and digging into its back so it looked like it had been caught. It comes from the idea of the antlers being a masculine thing which has actually ended up injuring it. I started making the sculpture with the head upright and because the clay was really wet it started falling further back. At one stage it has its head up, but as it started to move it seemed to became more real.
When I made the horses I wanted them to be sad creatures that would normally hold connotations of strength I also wanted them to look weak or like chess pieces, I just thought about it for a while and then I got the two ideas to work together.

I like Thomas Schütte, I like the fact that he makes sculpture then also does drawing. Somehow you can see that it's all by the same person even though it has all these different elements.

Interviewed by Gemma de Cruz

Caroline Warde, Peach Branch, 1998
painted resin, 40 x 90 x 90cm, courtesy the artist

Caroline Warde, Mule, 1998
painted resin, 90 x 90 x 60cm, courtesy the artist

cutesy images.

People often get other people to describe their work because it's a lot more eloquent.

Lost in Space I went along there and I was the only one who hadn't been to Goldsmiths, everyone else was really go-getting and I found that attitude hard to take. It's hard because it has become such a slaggable thing. I've found myself slagging it off. "YBA's, and it's just hype, media rubbish. It's all been leapt upon. It's so far removed from what's going on in people's studios. People are quietly getting on with things.

It's nice to keep things simple. There's so much guff that goes around when people talk about art and I don't see it like that. Art to me is really, really simple. How people relate to the world.

I did sculpture at college. I didn't do painting so I've come at it a different way.

I like making things. The whole hands on thing, which is why I went for sculpture as well.

I enjoy looking at them because I've made something I want to see.

Initially I was doing sculpture and making things and suddenly thought this is crazy. Because I was doing the drawing, then making the piece and really struggling with the making. I hated asking the technicians. I wanted to be self-sufficient. I did my MA at the Slade and the first piece was very similar to my degree show. That's when I thought "stop", I couldn't bear to

make another thing. Sculpture just seemed irrelevant. I started drawing on the walls and found it completely unrestricting. I could do whatever I wanted. That's how I started painting on walls.
But then, what was happening when it was for a show was that I had to come up with the goods *that* day. With the show at Karsten Schubert people were coming through with their work and I'd be there painting. I was there half an hour before the show opened thinking "This isn't working". It ended up being the complete opposite of what I wanted to be doing. I had an idea and wanted to do it. But to get it to work with all of the scale drawings etc. took any of the joy and continuity out of it.

The way that I paint them is the only way I can. I like things to be nice and have nice things around me. I don't like ugly things. That's why I make these images. To remind myself about nice things in the world. When I say *nice things*, it doesn't have to always be pretty.

They're all from images that are floating around in my head, and a lot of them I take from reference books. The nightingale, for example. I didn't know what a nightingale looked like but I knew I wanted to paint one so I looked it up, I was really pleased that it was quite a plain bird. It makes me think of kids illustration books I had when I was young and they're amazing, really evocative. I think there's something that relates back to that. The beads were taken from my window, I painted those sitting here.

I find it a lot easier to paint from a flat image. Even if I've got the actual object, I like to have the actual object and a flat image.

It seems to happen easier for me. Maybe because we're so tuned in to looking at photographic images nowadays.

I've often painted butterflies enjoy painting them and I'm getting better and better at it.

I like the line to pull you into the painting. Either a line from a left to

right diagonal or right to left.

I'm learning more and more to do something I like. When I get stuck in the murky depths of painting I do a butterfly and that takes me away from it. I see it as a pleasurable thing and that's what makes me want to do it.

That sounds airy fairy and simple, but it's things I want to see.

I build up thin glazes until I get the right colour. I don't just think of a colour and do it,

There are images that pop into my head.

these are done really quickly. Once I've got the background and the image in my head they can be done really quickly and that's part of the pleasure of it all. Seeing the image appear.

I do the background colour first and that usually dictates what the image is going to be. It can't be anything else. It has to be that particular thing. I really liked using the dark colours. Prussian blue and black mixed. I like the way it pulls things back, it works well with white, It can take on so many layers to get the brilliance, through, when it's with other colours. I didn't like it when I first did it.

I paint the grounds and once I've done that I match up the colours with what I'm going to be doing. I get as many coloured boards as I can, then match the colours to what I want to paint.

I try and get a space in the background. I don't want them to be seen like objects floating in space. I don't like paintings like that. A "Pretty Colour". Do you know the type of paintings I mean?

I was reading something recently about Dennis Potter. The article was saying that he died at the right time because his best work was the *singing detective* and he could never have done anything better.
I thought that must be awful to have done your best work 20 years ago and you can only repeat it or try again. I think that tells you something about life. It's not about doing "best" things. It's about the process and what you get from it.

I suppose that is when they work and when you look at a piece of work and you're left with something when you come away from it.

What I do is part of my life. It's not something separate I do. It all fits in to everything else in my life.

Interviewed by Gemma de Cruz

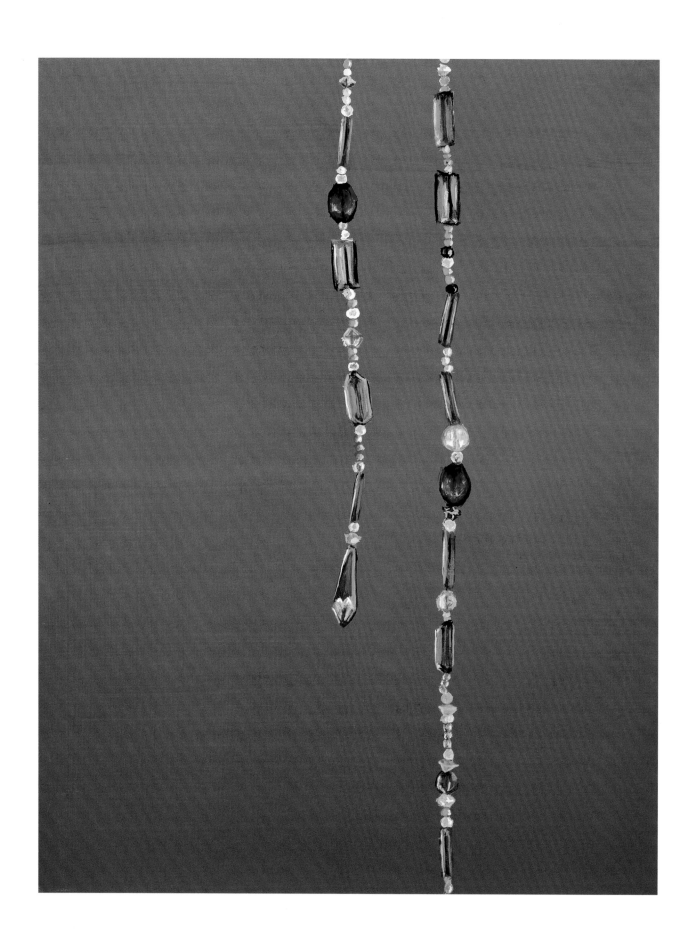

Jane Brennan, Beads, 1998
acrylic on wood, 22.9 x 17.8cm, courtesy the artist

Jane Brennan, Nightingale, 1998
acrylic on wood, 22.9 x 17.8cm, courtesy the artist

I love details.

I wanted to paint in a way that seemed very straightforward.

I wanted to describe something, without being too confessional or me, me, me.

The work is comic and funny and at the same time, it's serious and sad.

I wouldn't want them to just be funny and then you laugh, then don't think anything of them, or so gloomy, sad, "this is my world isn't it awful" teenage angsty expressionism. I think extremes of each of those models is something that would make me cringe. There is a plan but also it's incredibly instinctive. One painting tells you what the next one is you look at it and think I've made it too cartoony and I don't like that, I want them to be real in different kinds of ways. they're happy, sad, and there is a sense of realism.

I'm usually very specific. They're not in non-descript clothes, I am describing, a certain item of clothing that I like and want to see and think would be very funny to have in the painting the cropped top, tells you an awful lot about a person, you have seen it in adverts and you do know somebody who would wear it. It's like a trigger,

It seems like a very old-fashioned thing to say that the paintings reflect things that you're looking at. They reflect your direct experience.

I've given myself the complete freedom to choose any of the things I want to use from Art history and it's not a join the dots and spot where it's come from.

I do use elements of expressionism and I like it, I like how that's done, the colours, the sloppiness, I like the slapped on quality, the emotional appeal that has to the audience but no I'm not trying to be an expressionist.

if I've seen it and I like it and want to use it. I do

I think we take the fact that things are made from a wide range of different references as normal now,

I'm not interested in irony, why would I want to state the opposite of my intentions? I'm trying to do something which is quite clear, I'm trying to amalgamate details from my observations of daily life and the world around me with a knowledge of art history. I'm putting those two things together and I do not have a word for it but It's not ironic, it's not bad and it's not naive. It comes from a lot of looking and there is a lot of quotation in the paintings.

I've always had a passion for French 18th century painting,

Half the painting is a flat monochrome, which draws from the history of Malevich onwards.

So they use a lot of abstract painting language.

they're flat and they're brightly coloured,
In some paintings I want to pump up the narrative that's a bit forbidden at the moment and you find yourself embarrassed that you like this thing that you've thought you wouldn't like and always dismissed in the past.

I was upping things by suddenly working with narrative, and not being embarrassed about it, because narrative seemed like a hot potato. It seemed like an incredibly naïf thing. You could do narrative in photography, its all right for Jeff Wall to do narrative, or Cindy Sherman could do narrative, photography and narrative were fine but as soon as you tried to do narrative in painting... It's been over-done and over-abused, and it's very first year at art school. It's a difficult thing to bring back and not make it look terrible.

they had a

Poussin show at the Royal Academy.

I read it like it was completely contemporary. So then I thought I would do Poussin. I liked the fact that he was wierdly technicoloured, he had a lot of muscle-men and I thought that was kind of funny. The more I looked at him - he was just doing parties.

I wanted to do party paintings

My paintings have awkward drawing, but the awkward drawing's for a purpose. I know the length of people's arms and legs and heads, Sometimes I might give them a bigger hairstyle so that they're all hairstyle, but it's like summing somebody up.

by making their feet too small or their hands big too. It's taking an awkward pose, or awkward gestures and shining the spotlight on it. Painting is a very selective process.

I got Picasso later on in life and now I'm an evangelical Picasso fan. With Picasso he was daring himself to be ugly, he was making things that were sweet and pretty and also gut wrenchingly ugly.

I like Cy Twombly, Guston, Warhol, Matisse, the qualities in the painting and drawing, the topics.
I like German photography all the harsh German stuff. I like Baselitz
I like 70's Californian performance art people who were describing what it was like to go for a walk or have a cup of coffee. Sometimes when you're painting you find yourself making it look like a bit of something else, you paint a watch strap and it looks a bit like Guston and that's kind of exciting. You're never really sure if you are putting that in deliberately or not It's intelligent intuition.
I like Cindy Sherman everytime I look at them I think they're rich and complex.I like Mike Kelley I like the attitude, the idea of making trashy things upmarket or downmarket
I like artists who draw attention to their own creativity and I think Picasso does that. I think Mike Kelleylooks at the embarrassment of creativity, the effect of the hand how people make things and have the desire to be creative.
I want to make that clear in the painting that I have a desire to be creative not in a running around in silk scarves kind of way. You're responding to the design of things in the world and responding to beauty, in things that have been given to you or found accidentally,
There's a sense of being polite and a sense of not being polite and getting that balance right

You make a choice to do a certain kind of painting. I'm not trying to be cute. I'm not the Kylie Minogue of painting.

Interviewed by Gemma de Cruz

Martin Maloney, Hey Good Looking!
(After Poussin's The Choice of Hercules), 1998
oil on canvas, 244 x 335cm,
collection Saatchi Gallery, London/courtesy Anthony D'Offay Gallery, London

Steven Gontarski
Wednesday 9 September 1998

I'm using   modern things, modern looks,

I went to Brown university.

contemporary architecture , I didn't really design architecture. I just studied the history and criticism.

I started doing a little bit of architecture and some of the first artworks I did were architectural pieces. I was in to sewing as well. I was in to what happens when you have a flat form/pattern and you sew it up together and it becomes 3D. And that was through architecture

So, that's when I really started to get into this sort of thing. Since then I've been sewing because for me it was a very instant way to use contour lines to make a 3D form. And that's all in the sewing and basically having a 2D pattern. So that's where it started. Then in New York you live in a tiny little apartment and sewing was something I could do because you don't need so much space. I could sit in front of the TV on my couch and just sew something together when I came home from work.

I was making up forms more based on animals

Imaginary animals and real animals like dogs and things like that and they were sewn together then I started getting into human forms as well and at the time the look that I was going for was very crusty because at the time they were people I really looked at in New York. I tend to go through phases where I really look at a certain person and at the time I was into the tribal crusty people who lived in the East Village which was round the corner from where I lived. So you pass them every day and they hang around in packs in the park and they have a very specific look and I thought this is nice, and is universal; its extremely East Village. I wanted to figure out what they were doing. Like how I could use some of that look. The dog was actually a crusty dog or I wanted it to be a crusty dog and I made some forms, like human forms that were the crusties and then when I came to London I just continued doing that basically they just became a little more complex and abstract and larger and the look is different as well.

I'm not really into crusties any more & I don't see them around very much so I've moved on to a different kind of thing.

Last year I did a lot more work that had actual clothes like a football shirt and for me it was very much because the clothing or the bits of clothing, the colour or whatever equalled a certain kind of guy or a certain kind of person. For me to identify what that character was all about. I'm like ok, that's the sporty guy and it's like the Spice Girls each have that little thing so you know which spice they are. I thought the sculpture needed that.

So for the past year I haven't been as interested in that as I am with the form itself. What the form can do. So the forms have becomes much more complicated and I'm trying to make them simpler as well in the covering. The three that I'm making for the ICA are all going to be white pieces. So I'm trying to strip them down basically and just deal with the forms and gestures and I'm very happy with the shiny-ness and the plasticity so I'll keep up with that and concentrate on that.

it's skin even if it's fabric,   soft form that is still solid.   stripping things down to lines,

I like Henry Moore.
    Cindy Sherman.
    Mike Kelley
    Paul McCarthy
The whole California thing.
Matthew Barney
He's silly, but there's a gothic heaviness

I think about the Chapmans a lot.   I feel they are basically taking recognisable

things that on their own are simple.   There's a lot of tradition there.

it is about sex. What a nice balance sex is. It's peaceful and at the same time

it's frenetic and crazy. that's the balance I'm going for.

the first double piece I've done.

2 pieces that make it up. So this is called *wife*

It's the most figurative thing I've done.

this is a copy of Michelangelo's *Dying Slave* this is called "Lying Active".

So the reason why I made the dying slave is a) It's so sexy. The original is probably the most sexiest piece of art I've ever seen. Its very funny because in the original he has this little vest top kind of around his shoulders. I use a lot of things like socks and vest tops and things like that so when I saw dying slave I thought this was really the piece that was made for me. Then I liked the idea that every artist or band at some point does a cover version of something so I thought I'd very much like to do a cover version of something although it is Michelangelo.

Dying Slave is a piece that people recognise and it has some sort of history.
The whole point of a cover version is not to copy so you can't tell the original from the copy exactly. It's to be interpreted and re-defined that's what I'm trying to do.
I think, basically I'm reducing it for these three, for the dying slave his balls will probably stay pink and a little pink at the top. I think it is important to give it a feature. Because it's so figurative it doesn't need so many clues or anchors to bring it back in to something. Whereas with wife you do because a lot of forms are unrecognisable.

The way they're made is; I make an armature from wood, so it's a skeleton basically. The stuff over here is polyester wadding. You cut off a strip of it, wrap it around and sew it into place. It takes forever.

Sometimes it's difficult for me to look at the pieces. For example with the couple shagging. When I'm making it, it was un-sexy. There's nothing sexy about making it, but when you're all done and you leave it a while and the lighting is right the whole thing is just so sexy. I felt a gut feeling about that. Raw sumptuous. I was so happy that I got that from my piece.

I'm not an architect which is why I don't do drawings to plan out the form.

have an idea of what you want. All the design and all the shapes basically come out as I'm making
This goes back to my
interest in architecture and functionalism and artistry in the form. Glazing and windows, what you see is what you get. So I strip things down quite a lot using clear plastic lets you see the

seams. The clearness of it is about letting you see how it's made. I think a lot of the art in this is in the making and I think it becomes an intrinsic part of it.
There is a calmness in making it, but with a passion behind each piece. It would be nice if that came through. I'm not trying to be particularly clever, although they're not simple. I'm not trying to fool anybody. I want the overall look to be simple, light and easy, but there should be layers to it. I don't think by seeing the piece once just for five minutes that'll really do it and that'll mean anything much to you.
Basically I would like people to see in it what I'm putting in.

it's unfair to compare pop music and art although in terms of creating music & pop songs and creating a piece of art I do like to make these parallels because I very much like to hear reviews of new songs coming out and basically when you hear a critic reviewing something from a magazine who really knows what they're talking about musically, its fascinating to set up a list of criteria of how you judge a new song or whatever.
Is a song doing anything different. Yes or no? Did this song have to be made? What's the background what's different about the song? Does this artist mean it when he/she sings the song? These are all really good things and when I make art that's what I think.

Interviewed by Gemma de Cruz

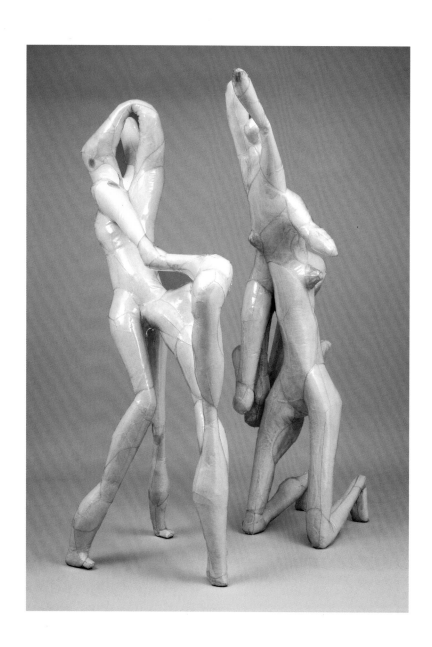

above:

Steven Gontarski, Wife, 1998

pvc, polyester wadding, synthetic hair and wood, 195 x 160 x 178cm
(width and depth have variable dimensions), collection Saatchi Gallery, London

right:

Steven Gontarski, Lying Active (Dying Captive), 1998

pvc, polyester wadding, synthetic hair and wood, 193 x 193 x 53cm,
collection Saatchi Gallery, London

Biographies

David Thorpe
Born in London, England, 1972

Education
1990 - 1991	Foundation Course, Chelsea School of Art and Design, London
1991 - 1994	BA Fine Art, Humberside University
1996 - 1998	MA Fine Art, Goldsmiths College, University of London

Selected Group Exhibitions
1996	Angels, Standpoint Gallery, London
1997	Need for Speed, Steirischer Herbst '97, Graz, Austria
	B.o.n.g.o., Bricks and Kicks Gallery, Vienna
	David Thorpe and Simon Hollington, City Racing Gallery,
1997 - 1998	David Thorpe and Simon Periton, Habitat, London
1998	Sociable Realism, Stephen Friedman Gallery, London
	Printemps I, Deutsch Britische Freundschaft, London
	Post-Neo Amateurism, Chisenhale Gallery, London
	Futures for the Young, Axel Mörner, Stockholm
	Sunshine Breakfast, Michael Janssen, Cologne
	Ruislip, De Praktijk Gallery, Amsterdam

Jun Hasegawa
Born in Mie, Japan, 1969

Education
1991 - 1992	Foundation Course, Wimbledon School of Art, London
1992 - 1995	BA Fine Art, Goldsmiths College, University of London

Selected Group Exhibitions
1995	Guess Who's Coming to Dinner, Lost in Space, London
	Multiple Orgasm, Lost in Space, London
	White Trash, Lost in Space, London
	Gothic, Lost in Space, London
1996	Face to Face, Victoria Miro Gallery, London
	New Contemporaries, Tate Gallery, Liverpool; Camden Art Centre, London
	Die Yuppie Scum, Karsten Schubert Gallery, London
	How will we behave?, Robert Prime Gallery, London
	Physiognomical Corpus, One in the Other, London
1997	Some Kind of Heaven, Kunsthalle Nürnberg, Germany; South London Gallery, London; John Hansard Gallery, Southampton; Cornerhouse, Manchester
	Multislot, The Basement, London
	Avatar, Entwistle Gallery, London
	Playing Dead, Spacex Gallery, Exeter
	Wrong Time, Wrong Place, Habitat Space, Habitat, London
1998	Printemps II, Deutsch Britische Freundschaft, London
	Dumbpop, Jerwood Gallery, London

Dexter Dalwood
Born in Bristol, England, 1960

Education
1981 - 1982	Foundation Course, St. Martin's School of Art and Design, London
1982 - 1985	BA Fine Art, St. Martin's School of Art and Design, London
1988 - 1990	MA Fine Art, Royal College of Art, London

Solo Exhibitions
1992	Clove Building, London
1995	Galerie Unwahr, Berlin

Selected Group Exhibitions
1992	Whitechapel Open, London
1993	Wild, IKON Gallery, Birmingham; Harris Museum, Preston
1994	Whitechapel Open, London
	Base, Salama-Caro Gallery, London
1995	John Moores 19, Walker Art Gallery, Liverpool
1996	Remaking Reality, Kettle's Yard, Cambridge
	Whitechapel Open, London
1997	Factory Place Open, Los Angeles, USA
	Thoughts, City Racing, London
1998	Humdrum (green), The Trade Apartment, London
	Fact and Fiction, IN ARCO, Turin, Italy

Peter Davies
Born in Edinburgh, Scotland, 1970

Education
1988 - 1989	Foundation Course, Central St Martin's College of Art and Design, London
1989 - 1992	BA Fine Art, University of Brighton
1994 - 1996	MA Fine Art, Goldsmiths College, University of London

Solo Exhibitions
1998	New Paintings, The Approach, London

Selected Group Exhibitions
1995	Guess Who's Coming to Dinner, Lost in Space, London
	Multiple Orgasm, Lost in Space, London
	White Trash, Lost in Space, London
	Gothic, Lost in Space, London
1996	Die Yuppie Scum, Karsten Schubert Gallery, London
1997	Artists and Their Spread, 53 Exmouth Market, London
	Sensation: Young British Artists from the Saatchi Collection, Royal Academy of Arts, London; Hamburger Bahnhof, Berlin
	Michael Craig-Martin, Ian Davenport, Peter Davies, Zebedee Jones, Michael Landy, Fiona Rae, Waddington Galleries, London
	Habitat Space, Habitat, London
1998	Home & Away, Gavin Brown's enterprise, New York